OUTWARD APPEARANCE

According to the Bible and the Spirit of Prophecy

R. Orce

INDEX

INTRODUCTION

Man's outward appearance is a subject considered in the Holy Scriptures from different perspectives and throughout different ages. This fact makes this topic quite extensive and rich in shades.

This study will only consider the aspects that refer to garments and hair among the people of God throughout the ages both in the Old and New Testament.

The subject of outward appearance is divided in two parts: Clothes and hair, with the purpose of giving a clearer view of the matter.

In order to present an objective view of this subject, comments will be brief and quotations from the Bible and the Spirit of Prophecy will be emphasized.

"And why take ye thought for raiment? Consider the lilies of the field, how they grow; they toil not, neither do they spin: and yet I say unto you, that even Solomon in all his glory was not arrayed like one of these. Wherefore, if God so clothe the grass of the field, which to day is, and to morrow is cast into the oven, shall he not much more clothe you, O ye of little faith?" Matthew 6:28-30. These words of the Lord Jesus clearly express the priority and characteristics of clothes in a very concise way, which we shall try to explain in the following pages.

CLOTHES

I.

I. Historical-Biblical Review

The Holy Scriptures present different perspectives of clothes, starting with their origin, evolution and purpose up to its symbolic sense in eternity.

We present here a panoramic chronology of clothes in the New and Old Testament.

1.1. Conceptual Chronology

Before man fell in sin, he did not wear any kind of clothes in the literal sense of the word, because it had not been considered necessary by his Creator. Man was surrounded by light.

"And they were both naked, the man and his wife, and were not ashamed." Genesis 2:25.

- **Introduction of sin**

"And the eyes of them both were opened, and they knew that they were naked; and they sewed fig leaves together, and made themselves aprons." Genesis 3:7.

"Adam and Eve both ate of the fruit, and obtained a knowledge which, had they obeyed God, they would never have had,--an experience in disobedience and disloyalty to God,--the knowledge that they were naked. The garment of innocence, a covering from God, which surrounded them, departed; and they supplied the place of this heavenly garment by sewing together fig leaves for aprons." *–Bible Commentary*, Vol. 1, p. 1084.

"This is the covering that the transgressors of the law of God have used since the days of Adam and Eve's disobedience. They have sewed together fig leaves to cover their nakedness, caused by transgression. The fig leaves represent the arguments used to cover disobedience. When the Lord calls the attention of men and women to the truth, the making of fig leaves into aprons will be begun, to hide the nakedness of the soul. But the nakedness of the sinner is not covered. All the arguments pieced together by all who have interested themselves in this flimsy work will come to naught (Ibid., Nov. 15, 1898)." –*Bible Commentary*, Vol. 1, p. 1084.

- **Expulsion from Paradise**

"Unto Adam also and to his wife did the Lord God make coats of skins, and clothed them." Genesis 3:21.

"In humility and inexpressible sadness Adam and Eve left the lovely garden wherein they had been so happy until they disobeyed the command of God. The atmosphere was changed. It was no longer unvarying as before the transgression. God clothed them with coats of skins to protect them from the sense of chilliness and then of heat to which they were exposed." –*The Story of Redemption*, p. 46.

- **Shame**

"And Shem and Japheth took a garment, and laid it upon both their shoulders, and went backward, and covered the nakedness of their father; and their faces were backward, and they saw not their father's nakedness." Genesis 9:23.

After the fall in sin, nakedness is considered in the Bible as a shame.

• Impersonation

"And Rebekah took goodly raiment of her eldest son Esau, which were with her in the house, and put them upon Jacob her younger son." Genesis 27:15.

With the purpose of impersonating Esau, Jacob wore the clothes of his elder brother to make his father believe that he was the firstborn.

• Well-being

"And Jacob vowed a vow, saying, If God will be with me, and will keep me in this way that I go, and will give me bread to eat, and raiment to put on, So that I come again to my father's house in peace; then shall the Lord be my God." Genesis 28:20, 21.

Clothes are a need for man and Jacob clearly expressed it in his covenant with God.

• Reform

"Then Jacob said unto his household, and to all that were with him, Put away the strange gods that are among you, and be clean, and change your garments." Genesis 35:2.

The instructions given by Jacob to the members of his family are very similar to the ones given in Sinai. Body hygiene and the change of clothes symbolize moral and spiritual purification of the mind and heart.

- **Sumptuousness**

"Now Israel loved Joseph more than all his children, because he was the son of his old age: and he made him a coat of many colours." Genesis 37:3.

Jacob publicly showed his preference for Joseph, being thus inconsiderate with his other children. He expressed this by giving him a costly coat. The consequences of such a deed were dramatic both for Joseph and Jacob.

"And they took Joseph's coat, and killed a kid of the goats, and dipped the coat in the blood; And they sent the coat of many colours, and they brought it to their father; and said, This have we found: know now whether it be thy son's coat or no." Genesis 37:31, 32.

- **Transformation**

"And she put her widow's garments off from her, and covered her with a veil, and wrapped herself, and sat in an open place, which is by the way to Timnath; for she saw that Shelah was grown, and she was not given unto him to wife. When Judah saw her, he thought her to be an harlot; because she had covered her face." Genesis 38:14, 15.

Tamar's change of clothes was the reason why she was considered someone totally different. From this quotation we can understand the great importance of outward appearance.

- **Identification**

"And it came to pass, when he heard that I lifted up my voice and cried, that he left his garment with me, and

fled, and got him out. And she laid up his garment by her, until his lord came home." Genesis 39:15, 16.

With the purpose of accusing Joseph, Potiphar's wife kept his clothes as a proof. This dramatic event illustrates the relation between a certain person and his clothes.

• Adaptability

"Then Pharaoh sent and called Joseph, and they brought him hastily out of the dungeon: and he shaved himself, and changed his raiment, and came in unto Pharaoh." Genesis 41:14.

The place, circumstances, people and events that surround a person have a direct influence upon the kind of clothes he wears.

• Social standard

"To all of them he gave each man changes of raiment; but to Benjamin he gave three hundred pieces of silver, and five changes of raiment." Genesis 45:22.

The possession of clothes in quantity and quality is a sign of a determined social standard or economical level.

"And the children of Israel did according to the word of Moses; and they borrowed of the Egyptians jewels of silver, and jewels of gold, and raiment." Exodus 12:35.

• Cleanliness

"And the Lord said unto Moses, Go unto the people, and sanctify them to day and to morrow, and let them wash their clothes." Exodus 19:10.

God would give His law three days later, therefore it was necessary to go through a thorough preparation, not only spiritual but also physical and material.

- **Covering**

"Neither shalt thou go up by steps unto mine altar, that thy nakedness be not discovered thereon." Exodus 20:26.

Coming in the presence of God requires modesty and sobriety since it is a solemn and reverent act.

- **Priestly service**

"But glory, honour, and peace, to every man that worketh good, to the Jew first, and also to the Gentiles." Romans 2:10.

"And thou shalt make holy garments for Aaron thy brother for glory and for beauty." Exodus 28:2.

The priestly garments had three main characteristics:

1. **Holiness**

"For this is the will of God, even your sanctification…" 1 Thessalonians 4:3.

2. **Honor**

"But glory, honour, and peace, to every man that worketh good…" Romans 2:10.

3. Beauty

"Give unto the Lord the glory due unto his name: bring an offering, and come before him: worship the Lord in the beauty of holiness" 1 Chronicles 16:29.

- ### Diversity

"And he shall put off his garments, and put on other garments, and carry forth the ashes without the camp unto a clean place." Leviticus 6:11.

The priests had to wear quite different clothes when they appeared before God and when they went about their common activities.

- ### Evidences

The Lord established in the clothes of each Israelite some unique elements that differentiated them from all other nationalities and identified them as members of God's people. The blue band and the fringes were two exclusive characteristics of the garments of every Hebrew.

"Speak unto the children of Israel, and bid them that they make them fringes in the borders of their garments throughout their generations, and that they put upon the fringe of the borders a ribband of blue: And it shall be unto you for a fringe, that ye may look upon it, and remember all the commandments of the Lord, and do them; and that ye seek not after your own heart and your own eyes, after which ye use to go a whoring: That ye may remember, and do all my commandments, and be holy unto your God." Numbers 15:38-40.

"Thou shalt make thee fringes upon the four quarters of thy vesture, wherewith thou coverest thyself." Deuteronomy 22:12.

God's purpose when establishing these distinctive signs was the following:

1. Observation

2. Remembrance of the law

3. Voluntary obedience

4. Renunciation of caprices and own ideas contrary to God's will

5. Renunciation of personal view contrary to God's will

6. Renunciation of incorrect actions

7. Holiness

- **Transference**

"And strip Aaron of his garments, and put them upon Eleazar his son: and Aaron shall be gathered unto his people, and shall die there." Numbers 20:26.

The garments of the High Priest were transferred from father to child because the latter would perform the same service to God and identify himself with the same faith and labor.

- Integration

"And seest among the captives a beautiful woman, and hast a desire unto her, that thou wouldest have her to thy wife; then thou shalt bring her home to thine house; and she shall shave her head, and pare her nails; and she shall put the raiment of her captivity from off her, and shall remain in thine house, and bewail her father and her mother a full month: and after that thou shalt go in unto her, and be her husband, and she shall be thy wife" Deuteronomy 21:11-13.

The integration of a foreigner to God's people and specifically of a captive woman required a complete change of her outward appearance, as shown in the Bible verse.

- **Differentiation**

"The woman shall not wear that which pertaineth unto a man, neither shall a man put on a woman's garment: for all that do so are abomination unto the Lord thy God." Deuteronomy 22.5.

The difference between man and woman was established by the Creator and entails also the way of dressing and the outward appearance.

The term *"abomination"* is best understood when one comprehends its immediate connotations, such as the following adjectives: detestable, execrable, loathsome and hateful.

These three variations: abominable, detestable and execrable are used to name the different degrees of excess of a bad thing or action and in this case *"abominable"* is even worse than detestable and it is parallel to execrable.

The term execrable refers mainly to the moral and religious area, while abominable and detestable refer to the former as well as to qualify something material.

It is interesting how the Holy Scriptures apply the same concept *"abomination"* to other human actions that are execrable for God:

"The graven images of their gods shall ye burn with fire: thou shalt not desire the silver or gold that is on them, nor take it unto thee, lest thou be snared therein: for it is an abomination to the Lord thy God. Neither shalt thou bring an abomination into thine house, lest thou be a cursed thing like it: but thou shalt utterly detest it, and thou shalt utterly abhor it; for it is a cursed thing" Deuteronomy 7:25, 26.

"When thou art come into the land which the Lord thy God giveth thee, thou shalt not learn to do after the abominations of those nations. There shall not be found among you any one that maketh his son or his daughter to pass through the fire, or that useth divination, or an observer of times, or an enchanter, or a witch, or a charmer, or a consulter with familiar spirits, or a wizard, or a necromancer. For all that do these things are an abomination unto the Lord: and because of these abominations the Lord thy God doth drive them out from before thee" Deuteronomy 18:9-12.

When we consider these Bible verses, we can better understand how the term *"abomination"* is not only used referring to an exchange of masculine and feminine garments but also to divination, astrology, idolatry and all sorts of spiritualistic acts.

- **Willingness**

"And in that day seven women shall take hold of one man, saying, We will eat our own bread, and wear our own apparel: only let us be called by thy name, to take away our reproach." Isaiah 4.1.

The Holy Scriptures mentions three kinds of duties of a husband. *"If he take him another wife; her food, her raiment, and her duty of marriage, shall he not diminish."* Exodus 21:10. One of these duties is to provide the necessary clothes, something that the women in Isaiah detest since they want to dress according to their own ideas and taste.

- **Worldliness**

"And it shall come to pass in the day of the Lord's sacrifice, that I will punish the princes, and the king's children, and all such as are clothed with strange apparel." Zephaniah 1:8.

Foreign customs in dressing were introduced among the people just as Isaiah describes it in 3:16-24, which completely contradicted the divine regulations on this matter, since the way the children of Israel dressed had to be a testimony that they belonged to God and of their high calling, as revealed in Numbers 15:37-41.

- **Simplicity and purity**

"In like manner also, that women adorn themselves in modest apparel, with shamefacedness and sobriety; not with broided hair, or gold, or pearls, or costly array; but (which becometh women professing godliness) with good works." 1 Timothy 2:9, 10.

Modesty, decency and chastity in dressing are characteristics of the appearance among the children of God.

- **Promise**

"He that overcometh, the same shall be clothed in white raiment; and I will not blot out his name out of the book of life, but I will confess his name before my Father, and before his angels." Revelation 3.5.

The Holy Scriptures explain the origin of the human being and also his future. Just as before the fall in sin, man was surrounded by a tunic of light, when the Lord Jesus comes to rescue the redeemed ones, He will dress them with white garments.

II. SYMBOLISM

This historical analysis of the clothes has helped us to understand its symbolism. This is what we shall present in this section in three fundamental aspects: sacerdotal, matrimonial and national.

2.1. Priesthood

The following quotations establish the relation between the literal priesthood in the Old Testament and the spiritual priesthood in the New Testament.

OLD TESTAMENT	NEW TESTAMENT
*"And take thou unto thee Aaron thy brother, and his sons with him, from among the children of Israel, that he may **minister unto me** in the priest's office, even Aaron, Nadab and Abihu, Eleazar and Ithamar, Aaron's sons. And thou shalt make **holy garments** for Aaron thy brother **for glory and for beauty."** Exodus 28:1, 2.	*"But ye are a chosen generation, **a royal priesthood**, an holy nation, a peculiar people; **that ye should show forth the praises of him who hath called you out of darkness into his marvellous light.**"*1 Peter 2:9.* "…hath made us kings and **priests unto God and his Father;** to him be glory and dominion for ever and ever." Revelation 1:6

It is important to understand very well the meaning of the sacerdotal garments in the Old Testament since God

Himself considered this matter as having great importance. This can be seen not only because this theme is presented in detail in two relatively long chapters in the Bible (Exodus 28:1-43; 39:1-31), but also because of the details of the description of each one of the parts of the garments.

GARMENT	PURPOSE	MEANING
"Holy garments" Exodus 28:2, 41.	"for glory and for beauty" "*…and shalt anoint them, and consecrate them, and sanctify them, that they may minister unto me…*"	**"Give unto the Lord the glory due unto his name**: bring an offering, and **come before him: worship the Lord in the beauty of holiness."** 1 Chronicles 16:29.
Ephod Exodus 28:6, 12.	'Memorial'	**"And did I choose him** out of all the tribes of Israel to be my priest, to offer upon mine altar, **to burn incense, to wear an ephod before me? And did I give unto the house of thy father all the offerings made by fire of the children of Israel?"** 1 Samuel 2:28.

GARMENT	PURPOSE	MEANING
Breastplate Exodus 28:15, 29, 30	Judgment upon his heart	"And the publican, standing afar off, would not lift up so much as his eyes unto heaven, but **smote upon his breast, saying, God be merciful to me a sinner.**" Luke 18:13.
Robe Exodus 28:31, 35.	*"will be upon Aaron to minister…"*	*"I will greatly rejoice in the Lord, my soul shall be joyful in my God; for **he hath clothed me with the garments of salvation, he hath covered me with the robe of righteousness…**"* Isaiah 60:10.
Plate Exodus 28:36, 37.	*"Holiness to the Lord"* *"the faults… grace before the Lord"*	*"Now these are **the commandments, the statutes, and the judgments, which …. And … they shall be as frontlets between thine eyes.**"* Deuteronomy 6:1, 8.

GARMENT	PURPOSE	MEANING
Coat Exodus 28:39-43	*"to minister"*	*"… **the oil of joy** for mourning, the garment of praise for the spirit of heaviness…"* Isaiah 61:3.
Mitre Exodus 28:39-43	*"to minister"*	*"Blessed is the man that endureth **temptation**: for when he is **tried**, he shall receive the **crown of life**, which the Lord hath promised to them that love him."* James 1:12.
Breeches Exodus 28:39-43	*"to minister"*	*"…covered their bodies…."* Ezekiel 1:11.

The seven basic elements of the priestly garments had the defined purpose of:

1. Serving the Lord

2. Honoring His name

3. Announcing the beauty of the truth

4. Reminding of the law of God

5. Reverencing God

6. Joy of salvation

7. Consecration

2.2. MARRIAGE

All along the Holy Scriptures, the symbol of marriage is used to depict the relation between God and His people, as we can see in the following verses:

"…for I have espoused you to one husband, that I may present you as a chaste virgin to Christ." 2 Corinthians 11:2.

"For the husband is the head of the wife, even as Christ is the head of the church: and he is the saviour of the body." Ephesians 5:23.

The poetic and symbolic description of the garments of the church is very beautiful and meaningful when compared to the characteristics of the priestly garments, such as:

"As I live, saith the Lord, thou shalt surely clothe thee with them all, as with an ornament, and bind them on thee, as a bride doeth." Isaiah 49:18.
"…a woman clothed with the sun, and the moon under her feet, and upon her head a crown of twelve stars." Revelation 12:1.
"Who is she that looketh forth as the morning, fair as the moon, clear as the sun, and terrible as an army with banners?" Song of Songs 6:10.

"Husbands, love your wives, even as Christ also loved the church, and gave himself for it; that he might sanctify and cleanse it with the washing of water by the word, that he might present it to himself a glorious church, not having spot, or wrinkle, or any such thing; but that it should be holy and without blemish." Ephesians 5:25-27.

"Let us be glad and rejoice, and give honour to him: for the marriage of the Lamb is come, and his wife hath made herself ready. And to her was granted that she should be arrayed in fine linen, clean and white: for the fine linen is the righteousness of saints." Revelation 19:7, 8.

PRIESTLY GARMENTS	GARMENTS OF THE CHURCH
*"**holy garments**"* *"for glory and for beauty"* *"… and shalt anoint them, and consecrate them, and sanctify them, that they may minister "* Exodus 28:2, 41	*"As I live, saith the Lord, thou shalt surely clothe thee with them all, **as with an ornament, and bind them on thee, as a bride doeth.**"* Isaiah 49:18. *"Husbands, love your wives, even as Christ also loved **the church**, and gave himself for it; that he might **sanctify and cleanse** it with the washing of water by the word, that he might present it to himself **a glorious church, not having spot, or wrinkle**, or any such thing; but that it should be **holy and without blemish.**"* Ephesians 5:25-27.

PRIESTLY GARMENTS	GARMENTS OF THE CHURCH
*"And thou shalt embroider the **coat of fine linen**."* Exodus 28:39.	*"Let us be glad and rejoice, and give honour to him: for the marriage of the Lamb is come, **and his wife hath made herself ready. And to her was granted that she should be arrayed in fine linen, clean and white: for the fine linen is the righteousness of saints"*** Revelation 19:7, 8.

In the same way that the Lord designed a priestly garment, he described the outward appearance of His people in a beautiful way, underlining the purity, holiness, inner beauty and brightness of His church like an immaculate virgin. The Lord, as the husband, takes upon Himself the responsibility of clothing her, according to Exodus 21:10.

2.3. NATIONAL

The Lord had foreseen that the appearance of Israel, as a nation, should be identified with its faith and should be a permanent declaration of it for each and every member of the chosen nation as well as for all other nations.

"That ye may remember, and do all my commandments, and be holy unto your God. I am the Lord your God, which brought you out of the land of Egypt, to be your God: I am the Lord your God." Numbers 15:40, 41.

"And the Lord hath avouched thee this day to be his peculiar people, as he hath promised thee, and that thou shouldest keep all his commandments; and to make thee high above all nations which he hath made, in praise, and in name, and in honour; and that thou mayest be an holy people unto the Lord thy God, as he hath spoken." Deuteronomy 26:18, 19.

The principles that differentiated Israel from all other nations, were expressed both in the common garments of each Hebrew as well as in the special garments of the priests.

The following diagram will help to understand the three levels presented:

NATION	INDIVIDUAL	PRIESTHOOD

NATION	INDIVIDUAL	PRIESTHOOD
"Speak unto the children of Israel, and bid them that they make them fringes in the borders of their garments throughout their generations, and that they put upon the fringe of the borders a ribband of blue." Numbers 15:38.	*"But ye are a chosen generation, a royal priesthood, an holy nation, a peculiar people..."* 1 Peter 2:9.	*"And thou shalt make holy garments for Aaron thy brother for glory and for beauty. And thou shalt speak unto all that are wise hearted, whom I have filled with the spirit of wisdom, that they may make Aaron's garments to consecrate him, that he may minister unto me in the priest's office."* Exodus 28:2, 3.
PURPOSE		
"...that ye may look upon it, and remember all the commandments of the Lord, and do them; ... and be holy unto your God." Numbers 15:39, 40.	*"... that ye should show forth the praises of him who hath called you out of darkness into his marvellous light."* 1 Peter 2:9.	*"...and shalt anoint them, and consecrate them, and sanctify them, that they may minister unto me in the priest's office."* Exodus 28:41.

Law of God
Announcement of the truth
Consecration

GARMENTS

Sanctification

III. APPLICATION

The following section has as a purpose to present the actual importance of garments.

3.1. Education

The topic of dress is not a secondary or superficial matter in Christian education, but a teaching that completes the educational process as seen in the following testimony:

"No education can be complete that does not teach right principles in regard to dress. Without such teaching, the work of education is too often retarded and perverted." – *Education*, p. 246.

The guidelines regarding the right way of dressing should not be based on subjective opinions or ideas, but the Holy Scriptures should establish the principles to be followed:

"All matters of dress should be strictly guarded, following closely the Bible rule. Fashion has been the goddess who has ruled the outside world, and she often insinuates herself into the church. The church should make the Word of God her standard, and parents should think intelligently upon this subject. When they see their children inclined to follow worldly fashions, they should, like Abraham, resolutely command their households after them. Instead of uniting with the world, connect them with God." –*Child Guidance*, p. 430.

The dress reform among the people of God pursues specific goals: comfort and distinction.

"To protect the people of God from the corrupting influence of the world, as well as to promote physical and moral health, the dress reform was introduced among us. It was not intended to be a yoke of bondage, but a blessing, not to increase labor, but to save labor, not to add to the expense of dress, but to save expense. It would distinguish God's people from the world and thus serve as a barrier against its fashions and follies. He who knows the end from the beginning, who understands our nature and our needs,--our compassionate Redeemer,--saw our dangers and difficulties, and condescended to give us timely warning and instruction concerning our habits of life, even in the proper selection of food and clothing." – *Counsels on Health*, p. 598.

3.2. Personal identity

Clothes are directly related to the person who wears them and identify him/her as such. The following verses will help us to understand this:

"And they sent the coat of many colours, and they brought it to their father; and said, this have we found: know now whether it be thy son's coat or no." Genesis 37:32.

"And when the blood of thy martyr Stephen was shed, I also was standing by, and consenting unto his death, and kept the raiment of them that slew him." Acts 22:20.

"And one of the elders answered, saying unto me, what are these which are arrayed in white robes? And whence came they?" Revelation 7:13.

The choice of clothes and the fact of wearing them help identify the characteristics that are innate to a person. Clothes give a distinctive message regarding the image a person wants to present.

"Love not the world, neither the things [that are] in the world. If any man love the world, the love of the Father is not in him." 1 John 2:15.

"Those who claim to know the truth and understand the great work to be done for this time are to consecrate themselves to God, soul, body, and spirit. In heart, in dress, in language, in every respect they are to be separate from the fashions and practices of the world. They are to be a peculiar and holy people. It is not their dress that makes them peculiar, but because they are a peculiar and holy people, they cannot carry the marks of likeness to the world." *–Fundamentals on Christian Education*, p. 311.

"But how are the professed people of God today maintaining the honor of His name? How could the world infer that they are a peculiar people? What evidence do they give of citizenship in heaven?

"Puritan plainness and simplicity should mark the dwellings and apparel of all who believe the solemn truths for this time... Our dress, our dwellings, our

conversation, should testify of our consecration to God."
–*God's Amazing Grace*, p. 344.

"The children of Israel, after they were brought out of Egypt, were commanded to have a simple ribbon of blue in the border of their garments, to distinguish them from the nations around them, and to signify that they were God's peculiar people. The people of God are not now required to have a special mark placed upon their garments. But in the New Testament we are often referred to ancient Israel as examples. If God gave such definite directions to his ancient people in regard to their dress, will not the dress of his people in this age come under his notice? Should there not be in their dress a distinction from that of the world? Should not the people of God, who are his peculiar treasure, seek even in their dress to glorify God? And should they not be examples in point of dress, and by their simple style rebuke the pride, vanity and extravagance of worldly, pleasure-loving professors? God requires this of his people." –*Selected Messages*, Book 2, p. 473.

3.3. Personal Condition

The clothes do not only identify the person in a certain way before others, but they also reveal their way of thinking and acting as well as their condition.

"And she had a garment of divers colours upon her: for with such robes were the king's daughters that were virgins appareled..." 1 Samuel 13:18.

"And she arose, and went away, and laid by her veil from her, and put on the garments of her widowhood." Genesis 38:19.

3.4. Differences between Sexes

"The woman shall not wear that which pertaineth unto a man, neither shall a man put on a woman's garment: for all that do so are abomination unto the Lord thy God" Deuteronomy 22:5.

"In this style of dress God's order has been reversed and His special directions disregarded. Deuteronomy 22:5: 'The woman shall not wear that which pertaineth unto a man, neither shall a man put on a woman's garment: for all that do so are abomination unto the Lord thy God.' God would not have His people adopt this style of dress. It is not modest apparel, and is not at all fitting for modest, humble women who profess to be Christ's followers. God's prohibitions are lightly regarded by all who advocate doing away with the distinction of dress between males and females." *–Testimonies for the Church*, p. 459.

"There is an increasing tendency to have women in their dress and appearance as near like the other sex as possible and to fashion their dress very much like that of men, but God pronounces it abomination. 'In like manner also, that women adorn themselves in modest apparel, with shamefacedness and sobriety.' 1 Timothy 2:9…

"God designed that there should be a plain distinction between the dress of men and women, and has considered the matter of sufficient importance to give explicit directions in regard to it; for the same dress worn by both sexes would cause confusion and great increase of crime." –*Child Guidance*, p. 427.

3.5. Mood

Generally the mood is visible through a person's outward appearance, by the colors worn, the way of dressing, etc. Clothes also show dramatic condition or circumstances.

"And the Lord said, like as my servant Isaiah hath walked naked and barefoot three years for a sign and wonder upon Egypt and upon Ethiopia." Isaiah 20:3.

"Therefore I will wail and howl, I will go stripped and naked: I will make a wailing like the dragons, and mourning as the owls." Micah 1:8.

"Then David arose from the earth, and washed, and anointed himself, and changed his apparel, and came into the house of the Lord, and worshipped: then he came to his own house; and when he required, they set bread before him, and he did eat." 2 Samuel 12:20.

3.6. To Confess God

"Consistency is a jewel. Our faith, our dress, and our deportment must be in harmony with the character of our work, the presentation of the most solemn message ever given to the world.

"Our work is to win men to belief of the truth, win by preaching and by example also, by living godly lives. The truth in all its bearings is to be acted, showing the consistency of faith with practice. The value of our faith will be shown by its fruit. The Lord can and will impress men by our intense earnestness. Our dress, our deportment, our conversation and the depth of a growing experience in spiritual lines, all are to show that the great principles of truth we are handling are a reality to us. Thus the truth is to be made impressive as a great whole and command the intellect. Truth, Bible truth, is to become the authority for the conscience and the love and life of the soul.--Letter 121, 1900." *–Evangelism*, pp. 541 542.

"Whosoever therefore shall confess me before men, him will I confess also before my Father which is in heaven. But whosoever shall deny me before men, him will I also deny before my Father which is in heaven." Matthew 10:32, 33.

"How is it? Are we confessing Christ in our daily life? Do we confess him in our dress, adorning ourselves with plain and modest apparel? Is our adorning that of the meek and quiet spirit which is of so great price in the sight of God? Are we seeking to advance the cause of the Master? Is the line of demarcation between you and the world distinct, or are you seeking to follow the fashions of this degenerate age? Is there no difference between you and the worldling? Does the same spirit work in you that works in the children of disobedience?" *–Review and Herald*, May 10, 1892

3.7. Conversion

"The idolatry of dress is a moral disease. It must not be taken over into the new life. In most cases submission to the gospel requirements will demand a decided change in the dress." –*Child Guidance*, p. 432.

"Evidence that the taste is converted will be seen in the dress of all who walk in the path cast up for the ransomed of the Lord." –*Acts of the Apostles*, p. 523.

"Those who, after receiving the truth, make no change in word or deportment, in dress or surroundings, are living to themselves, not to Christ. They have not been created anew in Christ Jesus, unto purification and holiness…" – *The Adventist Home*, p. 21.

"While we are to guard against needless adornment and display, we are in no case to be careless and indifferent in regard to outward appearance. All about our persons and our homes is to be neat and attractive. The youth are to be taught the importance of presenting an appearance above criticism, an appearance that honors God and the truth." – *The Adventist Home*, p. 22.

3.8. To Honor God

"In dress, as in all things else, it is our privilege to honor our Creator. He desires our clothing to be not only neat and healthful, but appropriate and becoming… Our appearance in every respect should be characterized by neatness, modesty, and purity…

"Our clothing, while modest and simple, should be of good quality, of becoming colors, and suited for service." –*Counsels to Parents, Teachers, and Students*, p. 302.

3.9. Evidence of the Character

"The dress and its arrangement upon the person are generally found to be the index of the man or the woman." –*Child Guidance*, p. 413.

"If they would have a saving influence, if they would have their lives tell in favor of the truth, let them imitate the humble Pattern. Let them show their faith by righteous works, and make the distinction broad between themselves and the world. The words, the dress, and the actions should tell for God. Then a holy influence will be shed upon all, and all will take knowledge of them, that they have been with Jesus. Unbelievers will see that faith in Christ's coming affects the character..." –*That I May Know Him*, p. 312.

"The external appearance is an index to the heart. When hearts are affected by the truth there will be a death to the world, and those who are dead to the world will not be moved by the laugh, the jeer, and the scorn of unbelievers. They will feel an anxious desire to be like their Master, separate from the world. They will not imitate its fashions or customs. The noble object will be ever before them, to glorify God and gain the immortal inheritance." –*That I May Know Him*, p. 312.

"Simplicity of dress will make a sensible woman appear to the best advantage. We judge of a person's character by the style of dress worn. A modest, godly woman will dress modestly. A refined taste, a cultivated mind, will be revealed in the choice of a simple, appropriate attire. The young women who break away from the slavery of fashion will be ornaments to society. The one who is simple and unpretending in her dress and in her manners shows that she understands that a true woman is characterized by moral worth. How charming, how interesting, is simplicity in dress, which in comeliness can be compared with the flowers of the field.--Review and Herald, November 17, 1904." –*Messages to Young People*, p. 353.

"There should be no carelessness in dress. For Christ's sake, whose witnesses we are, we should seek to make the best of our appearance. In the tabernacle service, God specified every detail concerning the garments of those who ministered before Him. Thus we are taught that He has a preference in regard to the dress of those who serve Him. Very specific were the directions given in regard to Aaron's robes, for his dress was symbolic. So the dress of Christ's followers should be symbolic. In all things we are to be representatives of Him. Our appearance in every respect should be characterized by neatness, modesty, and purity. But the Word of God gives no sanction to the making of changes in apparel merely for the sake of fashion,--that we may appear like the world. Christians are not to decorate the person with costly array or expensive ornaments." –*Evangelism*, p. 268.

"The words of Scripture in regard to dress should be carefully considered. We need to understand that which the Lord of heaven appreciates in even the dressing of the body. All who are in earnest in seeking for the grace of Christ will heed the precious words of instruction inspired by God. Even the style of the apparel will express the truth of the gospel." –*Evangelism*, p. 269.

3.10 Reflexion

"Our words, our actions, and our dress are daily, living preachers, gathering with Christ, or scattering abroad. This is no trivial matter, to be passed off with a jest. The subject of dress demands serious reflection and much prayer. Many unbelievers have felt that they were not doing right in permitting themselves to be slaves of fashion; but when they see some who make a high profession of godliness dressing as worldlings dress, enjoying frivolous society, they decide that there can be no wrong in such a course. Testimonies, vol. 4, p. 641. (1881)." – *Evangelism*, p. 673.

"My sisters, your dress is telling either in favor of Christ and the sacred truth or in favor of the world. Which is it?" –*Child Guidance*, p. 420.

"I was directed to the following scriptures. Said the angel, 'They are to instruct God's people.' 1 Timothy 2:9, 10: 'In like manner also that women adorn themselves in modest apparel, with shamefacedness and sobriety; not with broided hair, or gold, or pearls, or costly array; but (which becometh women professing godliness) with good works.' 1 Peter 3:3-5: 'Whose adorning let it not be that outward adorning of plaiting of the hair and of wearing of gold, or of putting on of apparel; but let it be the hidden man of the heart, in that which is not corruptible, even the ornament of a meek and quiet spirit, which is in the sight of God of great price. For after this manner in the old time the holy women also… adorned themselves.'" – *Child Guidance*, p. 416.

"Many look upon these injunctions as too old-fashioned to be worthy of notice; but He who gave them to His disciples understood the dangers from the love of dress in our time, and sent to us the note of warning. Will we heed the warning and be wise?" –*Child Guidance*, p. 416.

"Those who are truly seeking to follow Christ will have conscientious scruples in regard to the dress they wear; they will strive to meet the requirements of this injunction so plainly given by the Lord." –*The Youth's Instructor*, November 5, 1896.

"I would ask the youth of today who profess to believe present truth, wherein they deny self for the truth's sake. When they really desire an article of dress, or some ornament or convenience, do they lay the matter before the Lord in prayer to know if His Spirit would sanction this expenditure of means? In the preparation of their clothing, are they careful not to dishonor their profession of faith? Can they seek the Lord's blessing upon the time thus employed? It is one thing to join the church, and quite another thing to be united to Christ. Unconsecrated, world-loving professors of religion are one of the most serious causes of weakness in the church of Christ." – *Messages to Young People*, p. 357.

IV. GUIDING PRINCIPLES

The following twelve points summarize the main principles regarding dress.

4.1 To honor God

"In dress, as in all things else, it is our privilege to honor our Creator. He desires our clothing to be not only neat and healthful, but appropriate and becoming." *–Child Guidance*, p. 413.

4.2. Purity and Modesty

"Our appearance in every respect should be characterized by neatness, modesty, and purity… Our clothing, while modest and simple, should be of good quality, of becoming colors, and suited for service." *–Child Guidance*, pp. 413, 420.

4.3. Quality and Discretion

"Our clothing, while modest and simple, should be of good quality, of becoming colors, and suited for service. It should be chosen for durability rather than display. It should provide warmth and proper protection.

"The wise woman described in the Proverbs 'is not afraid of the snow for her household: for all her household are clothed with double garments." *–Child Guidance*, p. 420.

4.4. Cleanliness

"Our dress should be cleanly. Uncleanliness in dress is unhealthful, and thus defiling to the body and to the soul. 'Ye are the temple of God… If any man defile the temple of God, him shall God destroy.' 1 Cor. 3:16, 17." – *Messages to Young People*, p. 352.

4.5. Health

"In all respects the dress should be healthful. 'Above all things,' God desires us to 'be in health'--health of body and of soul. And we are to be workers together with Him for the health of both soul and body. Both are promoted by healthful dress." –*Child Guidance*, p. 398.

4.6. Simplicity and beauty

"It should have the grace, the beauty, the appropriateness, of natural simplicity. Christ has warned us against the pride of life, but not against its grace and natural beauty. He pointed to the flowers of the field, to the lily unfolding in its purity, and said, 'Even Solomon in all his glory was not arrayed like one of these.' Matthew 6:29. Thus by the things of nature, Christ illustrates the beauty that heaven values, the modest grace, the simplicity, the purity, the appropriateness, that would make our attire pleasing to Him." –*Counsels to Parents, Teachers, and Students*, p. 303.

4.7. Sobriety

"Let our sisters dress plainly, as many do, having the dress of good, durable material, appropriate for this age, and let not the dress question fill the mind. Our sisters should dress with simplicity. They should clothe themselves in modest apparel, with shamefacedness and sobriety. Give to the world a living illustration of the inward adorning of the grace of God." *–Child Guidance*, p. 414.

4.8. Colors

"Taste should be manifested as to colors. Uniformity in this respect is desirable as far as convenient. Complexion, however, may be taken into account. Modest colors should be sought for. When figured material is used, figures that are large and fiery, showing vanity and shallow pride in those who choose them, should be avoided. And a fantastic taste in putting on different colors is bad." *–Child Guidance*, p. 420.

4.9. Reflection

"We should dress neatly and tastefully; but, my sisters, when you are buying and making your own and your children's clothing, think of the work in the Lord's vineyard that is still waiting to be done." *–Child Guidance*, p. 420.

4.10. Economy

"Practice economy in your outlay of means for dress. Remember that what you wear is constantly exerting an influence upon those with whom you come in contact. Do not lavish upon yourselves means that is greatly needed elsewhere. Do not spend the Lord's money to gratify a taste for expensive clothing." *–Child Guidance*, p. 421.

4.11. Easily fitting clothes

"The dress should fit easily, obstructing neither the circulation of the blood nor a free, full, natural respiration. The feet should be suitably protected from cold and damp. Clad in this way, we can take exercise in the open air, even in the dew of morning or evening, or after a fall of rain or snow, without fear of taking cold." – *Child Guidance*, p. 425.

4.12 Difference of sexes

"In like manner also, that women adorn themselves in modest apparel, with shamefacedness and sobriety.' 1 Timothy 2:9…

"God designed that there should be a plain distinction between the dress of men and women, and has considered the matter of sufficient importance to give explicit directions in regard to it; for the same dress worn by both sexes would cause confusion and great increase of crime." *–Child Guidance*, p. 427.

II.

HAIR

V. HISTORICAL-BIBLICAL REVIEW

The Holy Scriptures speak about the way the hair should be considered both by men and women, therefore we shall present some of these aspects in chronological order.

5.1. Conceptual chronology

- **Styling of hair**

The first Bible reference regarding hair is in relation with Joseph and his call to come before the Pharaoh.

"Then Pharaoh sent and called Joseph, and they brought him hastily out of the dungeon: and he shaved himself, and changed his raiment, and came in unto Pharaoh." Genesis 41:14.

After having being in prison for a certain time, it was necessary for Joseph to improve his outward appearance and one aspect was to have a hair-cut.

- **Purification**

"But it shall be on the seventh day, that he shall shave all his hair off his head and his beard and his eyebrows, even all his hair he shall shave off: and he shall wash his clothes, also he shall wash his flesh in water, and he shall be clean." Leviticus 14:9.

As an evidence of cleanliness and health it was necessary for the leper who was now healthy to finish with the whole process of purification by completing shaving off all the hair in his body since now he would begin a new life.

- **Shape**
"Ye shall not round the corners of your heads, neither shalt thou mar the corners of thy beard" Leviticus 19:27.

According to this Bible verse it is not permitted to cut the hair or the beard in a certain shape. One should respect the natural way in which they grow.

- **Vow**
"All the days of the vow of his separation there shall no razor come upon his head: until the days be fulfilled, in the which he separateth himself unto the Lord, he shall be holy, and shall let the locks of the hair of his head grow." Numbers 6:5.

One of the sign of the vow of a Nazarene was to be seen in his hair that was allowed to grow for a certain time in the case of a partial vow, or for the whole life, a per life vow.

- **Shaving**
"Ye are the children of the Lord your God: ye shall not cut yourselves, nor make any baldness between your eyes for the dead." Deuteronomy 14:1.

To shave off the hair either partially or totally was absolutely forbidden as we read in Leviticus 21:5: *"They shall not make baldness upon their head, neither shall they shave off the corner of their beard."* "*...nor make themselves bald for them*" Jeremiah 16:6.

- **Woman's hair**

"*... thy hair is as a flock of goats that appear from Gilead.*" Song of Songs 6:5.

"*Thine head upon thee is like Carmel, and the hair of thine head like purple; the king is held in the galleries.*" Song of Songs 7:5.

The ideal that we see in Song of Songs is a woman with long hair.

- **Shame**

"*Therefore the Lord will smite with a scab the crown of the head of the daughters of Zion, and the Lord will discover their secret parts.*" Isaiah 3:17.

Women had to shave their hair off because of sickness or as a sign of shame when invaders destroyed their country.

- **Deep sorrow**

"*And in that day did the Lord God of hosts call to weeping, and to mourning, and to baldness, and to girding with sackcloth.*" Isaiah 22.12.

To shave the hair off is a sign of deep sorrow and dramatic circumstances.

- **Rejection**

"Cut off thine hair, O Jerusalem, and cast it away, and take up a lamentation on high places; for the Lord hath rejected and forsaken the generation of his wrath." Jeremiah 7:29.

Both the verb and the possessive adjective *"thine"* are in Hebrew in the feminine form. This is evidence that the message is addressed to a woman, without a doubt to Jerusalem. The fact that a woman is commanded to cut off her hair is an evidence of the abhorrence and abandonment from the side of God.

- **Frontal shave**

"Egypt, and Judah, and Edom, and the children of Ammon, and Moab, and all that are in the utmost corners, that dwell in the wilderness: for all these nations are uncircumcised, and all the house of Israel are uncircumcised in the heart." Jeremiah 9:26.

Literally *"all that are in the utmost corners"*, which means *"those who shave their temples."* Some people, like the tribe of Cedar, in the north of Arabia, had the custom of shaving their hair around the temples.

- **A man's hair**

"Neither shall they shave their heads, nor suffer their locks to grow long; they shall only poll their heads." Ezekiel 44:20.

The Lord clearly prescribed that a man should not shave or let his hair long and disorderly indefinitely, but he had to have it cut and carry it orderly.

- **Color**

"Neither shalt thou swear by thy head, because thou canst not make one hair white or black." Matthew 5:36.

The Lord has not authorized any human being to change the color of his hair since it is not possible to do it naturally and it is not permitted to do it artificially.

VI. SYMBOLISM

In a man's and a woman's appearance, the hair-style is included. This also has a symbolic biblical meaning.

6.1. Male

In the New Testament, it is clearly presented the position of the Christian church regarding hair. In relation to a man, the principle and its symbolism are made clear.

Principle

"Doth not even nature itself teach you, that, if a man have long hair, it is a shame unto him?" 1 Corinthians 11:14.

1 Reason *"...the head of every man is Christ..."* 1 Corinthians 11:3.

2 Reason *"...he is the image and glory of God."* 1 Corinthians 11:7.

6.2 Female

"And they had hair as the hair of women..." Revelation 9:8.

The Holy Scriptures presents the hair of a woman as a sign of identification.

Principle

"But if a woman have long hair, it is a glory to her…" 1 Corinthians 11:15.

1 Reason   *"the head of the woman is the man…"* 1 Corinthians 11:3.

2 Reason   *"…because of the angels"* 1 Corinthians 11:10.

The following diagram summarizes these ideas.

HAIR	
MAN	WOMAN
Short 1 Corinthians 11:14	Long 1 Corinthians 11:15
DIFFERENCES BETWEEN SEXES	

<table>
<tr>
<td>"… the head of every man is Christ"

"… he is the image and glory of God"
1 Corinthians 11:3, 7.</td>
<td>C
H
R
I
S
T</td>
<td>"…the head of the woman is the man…"

"…because of the angels."
1 Corinthians 11:3, 10.</td>
</tr>
</table>

VI. APPLICATION AND PRINCIPLES

It is very important to understand the practical aspect of this subject. Therefore, a series of principles are presented on this regard.

6.1. Shape

"Ye shall not round the corners of your heads, neither shalt thou mar the corners of thy beard." Leviticus 19:27.

"They shall not make baldness upon their head, neither shall they shave off the corner of their beard…" Leviticus 21:5.

"…nor make any baldness…" Deuteronomy 14:1.

"…all that are in the utmost corners…" Jeremiah 9:26.

"….not with braided hair…" 1 Timothy 2:9.

"…let it not be that outward adorning of plaiting the hair…" 1 Peter 3:3.

6.2 Color

"Neither shalt thou swear by thy head, because thou canst not make one hair white or black" Matthew 5:36.

6.3 Style

"Doth not even nature itself teach you, that, if a man have long hair, it is a shame unto him? But if a woman have long hair, it is a glory to her: for her hair is given her for a covering." 1 Corinthians 11:14, 15.

VIII. BIBLIOGRAPHY

Ellen G. White's

AG Amazing Grace
AH Adventist Home
BC Bible Commentary
CG Child Guidance
CH Counsels on Health
CT Counsels to Teachers, Parents and Students
Ed. Education
Ev. Evangelism
FE Fundamentals of Christian Education
GC The Great Controversy
MYP Messages to Young People
RH Review and Herald
SM Selected Messages
SR The Story of Redemption
T Testimonies
TMK That I May Know Him